Paul Simon.

Mother And Child Reunion

Words and Music by PAUL SIMON

Duncan

Words and Music by PAUL SIMON

Moderately slow and steady

mp

mf

Em   D

1. Coup-le in the next____ room   bound to win a prize,____   They've been

G   A   D   C   G

go - in' at it all____ night____ long,   Well, I'm tryin' to get some sleep, but these

C   G   C   G

mo - tel walls are cheap, -   Lin - coln Dun - can is____ my name and here's my

song,_____ here's my song.

2. My fath - er was a fish - er - man, my ma-ma was a fish - er - man's friend, And

I was born in the bore - dom and the chow - der, So

when I reached my prime, I left my home in the Mar - i - times,__

Head - ed down the turn - pike for New Eng - land, ___ sweet New Eng - land.

Instrumental solo

3. Holes in my con - fi - dence, ___ holes in the knees of my jeans, I's

Everything Put Together Falls Apart

Words and Music by PAUL SIMON

Run That Body Down

Words and Music by PAUL SIMON

Me And Julio Down By The Schoolyard

Words and Music by PAUL SIMON

Armistice Day

Words and Music by PAUL SIMON

Peace Like A River

Words and Music by PAUL SIMON

Papa Hobo

Words and Music by PAUL SIMON

Moderately slow

Mm _____ It's

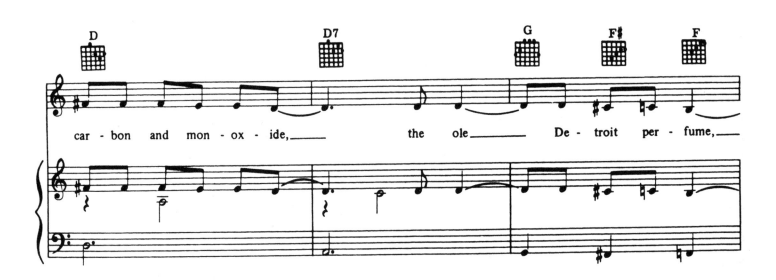

car - bon and mon - ox - ide, ____ the ole ____ De - troit per - fume, ____

Hobo's Blues

Music by PAUL SIMON and STEPHANE GRAPPELLI

Moderately, with a bounce
Instrumental Solo

Paranoia Blues

Words and Music by PAUL SIMON

I just got out in the nick of time.___ Once I was down in Chi - na town,

I was eat - in' some Lin's chow fon,___

I hap - pened to turn a - round,___ And when I

looked I seen my chow fon's gone.___ Oh no, no,___

Congratulations

Words and Music by PAUL SIMON

Moderately slow

Con - gra - tu - la - tions!   Oh, ___

___ seems like you've done it a - gain,   And

I ain't had ___ such ___ mis - e - ry ___   since

59

There Goes Rhymin' Simon.

Kodachrome™

Words and Music by PAUL SIMON

* "KODACHROME" is a registered trademark for color film.

cam - 'ra, I love to take a pho - to - graph, ___ So mom - ma, don't take ___

___ my Ko - da - chrome ___ a - way. ___

To next strain

No chord

Fine

2. If you took all ___

Verse 2.

___ the girls ___ I knew when I was sin - gle

Something So Right

Words and Music by PAUL SIMON

Tenderness

Words and Music by PAUL SIMON

Take Me To The Mardi Gras

Words and Music by PAUL SIMON

American Tune

Words and Music by PAUL SIMON

One Man's Ceiling Is Another Man's Floor

Words and Music by PAUL SIMON

thought I heard some-bod-y call my name.

Was A Sunny Day

Words and Music by PAUL SIMON

St. Judy's Comet

Words and Music by PAUL SIMON

Oo, lit - tle sleep - y boy,— do you know what time it is?___ Well, the

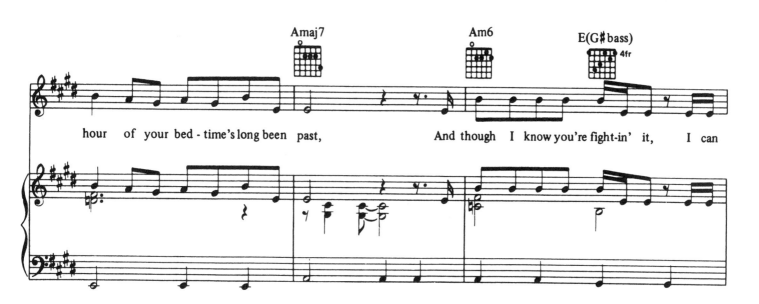

hour of your bed - time's long been past, And though I know you're fight-in' it, I can

104

Learn How To Fall

Words and Music by PAUL SIMON

You got to drift in   the breeze   be - fore you

set your sails,___   Oh, it's an oc - cu - pa - tion where the

wind pre - vails,_   Be - fore you set your sails,___   Drift in   the breeze.

Loves Me Like A Rock

Words and Music by PAUL SIMON

With a moving shuffle beat

mf

1. When I was a lit-tle boy,___ (When I was just a boy.) and the dev-il would call my

name, (When I___ was just a boy.) I'd say, "Now who do,___

who do you think you're fool-ing?"(When I___ was just a boy.) I'm a con - se -crat - ed

Rock. She rocks me like the rock of a - ges and loves me.

me. She love me, love me, love me, love me.

3. And if I was the Pres - i - dent, (Was the Pres - i -

dent.) the min - ute the Con - gress call my name. (Was the Pres - i -

Hearts And Bones.

Allergies

Words and Music by PAUL SIMON

Hearts And Bones

Words and Music by PAUL SIMON

One and one-half wan - der - ing Jews,___
back to__ the sea - son be - fore,___
One and one-half wan - der - ing Jews___

free to wan - der wher - ev - er___ they
look - ing back__ through the cracks in__ the
re - turned__ to their nat - u - ral

why, _____ why won't_ you love me ___ for

who I ___ am where I am?" _____

He said, "'Cause that's not the way the world is, __ ba-

by. ___

This is how_ I love___

When Numbers Get Serious

Words and Music by PAUL SIMON

I have a num-ber in my____ head, though I don't know why it's
ty - two. Four times four is for - ty -
____ me do in the shel - ter of your

there. When num - bers get se -
four. When num - bers get se -
arms. I am ev - er your vol -

ri - ous you see their shape ev - 'ry - where.____
ri - ous they leave a mark on your door.____
un - teer. I won't do you an - y harm.____

Think Too Much (b)

Words and Music by PAUL SIMON

The smart - est peo - ple_____ in___ the world_____
They say the left side_____ of___ the brain_____

Song About The Moon

Words and Music by PAUL SIMON

Mmm. _____ Mmm. _____

If you want to write a song a-bout the moon, _____
want to write a song a-bout the heart, _____
think a-bout a pho-to-graph _____ that you

walk a-long the cra-ters of the af-ter-noon,
think a-bout the moon be-fore you start,
real-ly can't re-mem-ber but you can't e-rase.

Train In The Distance

Words and Music by PAUL SIMON

Think Too Much (a)

Words and Music by PAUL SIMON

162

Rene And Georgette Magritte
With Their Dog After The War

Words and Music by PAUL SIMON

Cars Are Cars

Words and Music by PAUL SIMON

The Late, Great Johnny Ace

Words and Music by PAUL SIMON
Coda by PHILIP GLASS

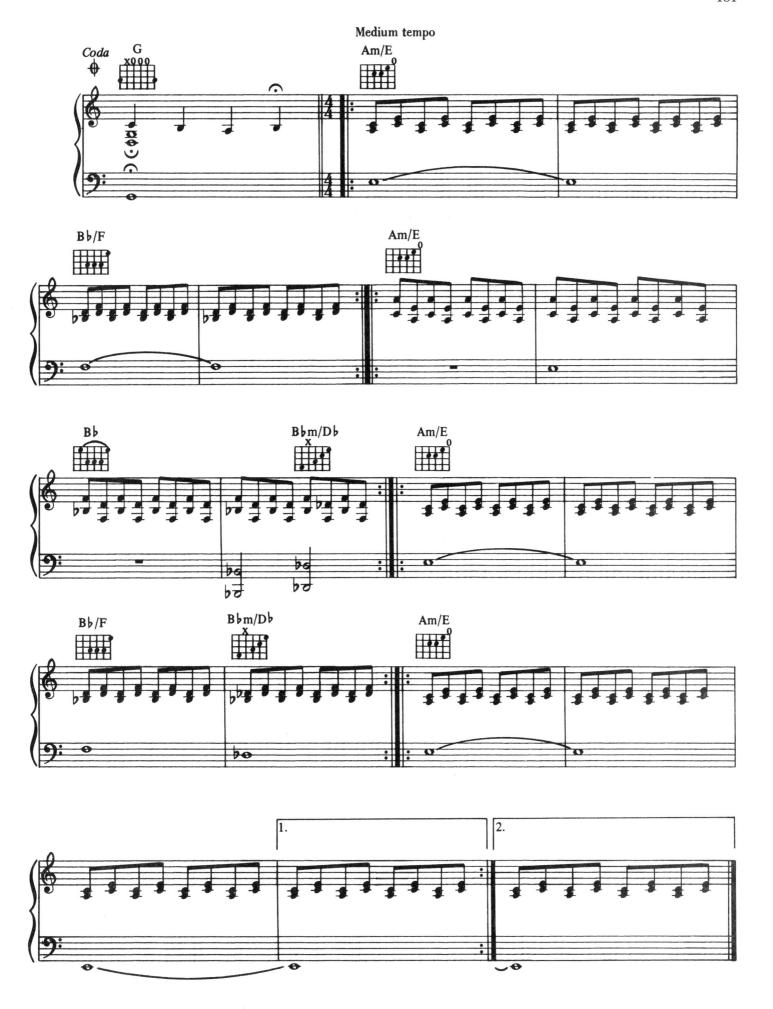

Graceland.

PAUL · SIMON
GRACELAND

184

Diamonds On The Soles Of Her Shoes

Words and Music by PAUL SIMON
Beginning by PAUL SIMON and JOSEPH SHABALALA

189

The Boy In The Bubble

Words by PAUL SIMON
Music by PAUL SIMON and FORERE MOTLOHELOA

Graceland

Words and Music by PAUL SIMON

I Know What I Know

Words by PAUL SIMON
Music by PAUL SIMON and GENERAL M.D. SHIRINDA

She

looked me o - ver and I guess she thought I was all right,
some - thing a - bout you that real - ly re - minds me of mon - ey."
moved so eas - i - ly, all I could think of was sun - light.

all
She was the
I said,

Gumboots

Words by PAUL SIMON
Music by PAUL SIMON and JOHNSON MKHALALI

It was in the ear - ly morn - ing hours when I fell in - to a
I was hav - ing this dis - cus - sion in a tax - i head - ing
I was walk - ing down the street when I thought I heard this

down - town,___
phone call.___
voice say,___

re - ar - rang - ing my po -
Be - liev - ing I had su - per - nat - u - ral
"Say, ain't we walk - in' down the

You don't feel you could love — me, but I feel you could.

You don't feel you could love —

— me, but I feel you could.

You don't feel you could love— me, but I feel you

could.

D.S. 𝄋 *(lyric 1) and fade*

You Can Call Me Al

Words and Music by PAUL SIMON

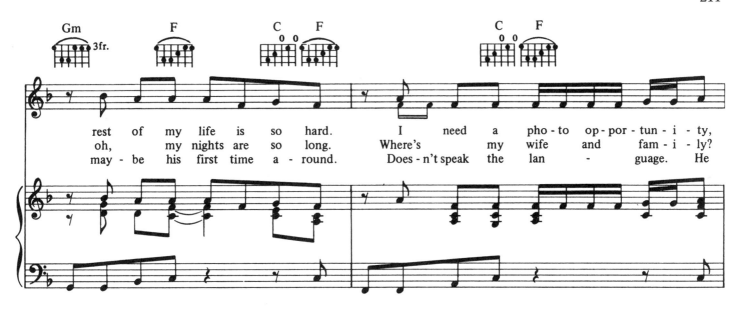

rest of my life is so hard.
oh, my nights are so long.
may-be his first time a - round.

I need a pho-to op-por-tun-i-ty,
Where's my wife and fam-i-ly?
Does-n't speak the lan - guage. He

I want a shot at re-demp-tion.
What if I die here?
holds no cur-ren-cy.

Don't want to end up a car-toon in a
Who'll be my role mod-el
He is a for-eign man.

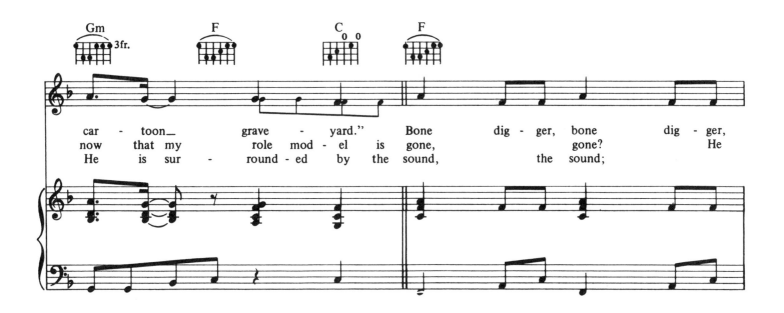

car-toon_ grave-yard." Bone dig-ger, bone dig-ger,
now that my role mod-el is gone, gone? He
He is sur-round-ed by the sound, the sound;

Under African Skies

Words and Music by PAUL SIMON

and the roots of rhy-thm re - main._____

In

Ka - oom - ba oom - ba

oom - ba oh._____

Ka -

220

Homeless

Words and Music by PAUL SIMON and JOSEPH SHABALALA

Home - less,— home - less.— Moon - light sleep - ing on a

mid - night lake.— Home - less,— home - less.—

Moon - light sleep - ing on a mid - night lake.— We are home - less,— we are

home - less.— The moon - light sleep - ing on a mid - night lake.— And we are

home - less,__ home-less, home - less.__ The moon-light sleep - ing on a

mid - night lake. Zi - o ya - mi zi - o ya - mi n-hli-zi-yo ya - mi n-hli-

zi - yo ya - mi a-ma-kha-za asengi bu-le-le n-hli-zi-yo ya - mi n-hli-

zi - yo ya - mi n-hli-zi-yo ya - mi angi-bu-le-le a-ma-kha-za n-hli-

loo loo___ too loo loo___ too loo loo loo___ loo loo loo

loo loo loo.___ Strong wind___ de-stroy our___ home.___

Man - y dead___ to - night, it could be you.___ Strong wind___ de-

stroy our___ home.___ Man - y dead___ to - night, it could be you.___ And we are

Crazy Love, Vol. II

Words and Music by PAUL SIMON

That Was Your Mother

Words and Music by PAUL SIMON

fa - yette,　　state of　Lou - i - si - an - a,　　　　　won-d'ring where a
fa - yette,　　state of　Lou - i - si - an - a,　　　　　won-d'ring what a
fa - yette,　a - cross the　street from the Pub - lic,　head - ing down to the

cit - y　boy__ could go_____　　　　　　to get a lit - tle con - ver - sa -
cit - y　boy__ could do_____　　　　　　to get her in a con - ver - sa -
Lone Star Ca - fe._____　　　　　　　May - be get a lit - tle con - ver - sa -

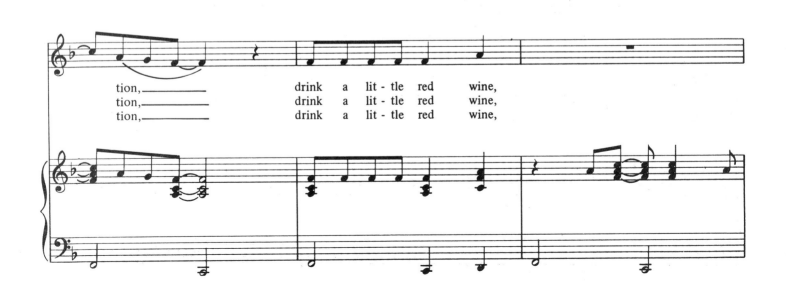

tion,_____　　drink a lit - tle red　wine,
tion,_____　　drink a lit - tle red　wine,
tion,_____　　drink a lit - tle red　wine,

catch a lit - tle bit of those Ca - jun girls__ danc - ing to Zy - de - co.__
dance to the mu - sic of Clif - ton Chen-ier, the King of the Ba - you.__
stand - ing in the shad - ow of Clif - ton Chen-ier danc - ing the night a - way.__

A - long__ comes a
Well, that__ was your

All Around The World
Or The Myth Of Fingerprints

Words and Music by PAUL SIMON

O - ver the moun - tain, down_ in the val - ley, lives a for - mer talk -
Out in the In - di - an O - cean some - where, there's a for - mer ar -
O - ver the moun - tain, down_ in the val - ley, lives the for - mer talk -

show host.__ Ev - 'ry - bod - y knows his name.___
my post, a - ban - doned now just like the war.___
show host.__ Far and wide his name was known.___